THE BIG BOOK OF

MAN-MADE WONDERS

BRIAN WILLIAMS

HAMLYN

The Big Book of Man-Made Wonders was
produced for Hamlyn Children's Books
by Lionheart Books, London

Published in 1993 by
Hamlyn Children's Books.
Part of Reed International Books Limited.
Michelin House, 81 Fulham Road.
London SW3 6RB

ISBN 0 600 57361 3

Printed in Italy

CONTENTS

RIVALLING MOUNTAINS

Aliens on a flying visit over our planet might marvel at its natural features – mountains, valleys, rivers, and seas. They might also wonder at the variety of towers and skyscrapers, dams and bridges, temples and tombs built on Earth.

In the past 10,000 years human ingenuity has created many truly amazing structures. Some of these have lasted for centuries. Others are more recent – the products of our modern world's concrete and steel technology.

FROM WANDERERS TO BUILDERS
Prehistoric human beings were wanderers. But from about 10,000 years ago people began to settle down and to build. At first, they became farmers, living in villages. In time the villages grew into towns, which were fortified by stone walls and towers, and the towns grew into city-states. Their rulers erected stone buildings as symbols of their power: palaces, fortresses, temples to the gods, and royal tombs to their own memories.

But civilizations come and go, and with them the towers and palaces of a new era rise on the rubble of the vanished spendours of the past. Beneath the traffic-filled streets of modern Mexico City lie the ruins of Tenochtitlan, lost capital of the Aztec Empire. Outside Cairo, the busy capital of Egypt, tourists marvel at a sight that has impressed travellers for 5,000 years – the Pyramids. Their majesty is enhanced by mystery, for the society that created these artificial mountains has long since gone. Only their mighty works remain, to fill succeeding generations with wonder.

Above: The Pyramids at Giza were built for the Pharaohs Khufu (Cheops), Khefren, and Menkure. How they were made is still largely a mystery. The builders seem to have used advanced mathematics backed by the muscle-power of 100,000 slave-workers.

Right: The masonry skill of the Pyramid builders is astonishing. Their massive blocks fit together so snugly that a knife blade will not slide between them. The entrance to Khufu's Pyramid is 18 m above ground. A sloping corridor led to the burial chambers – which may or may not have been occupied.

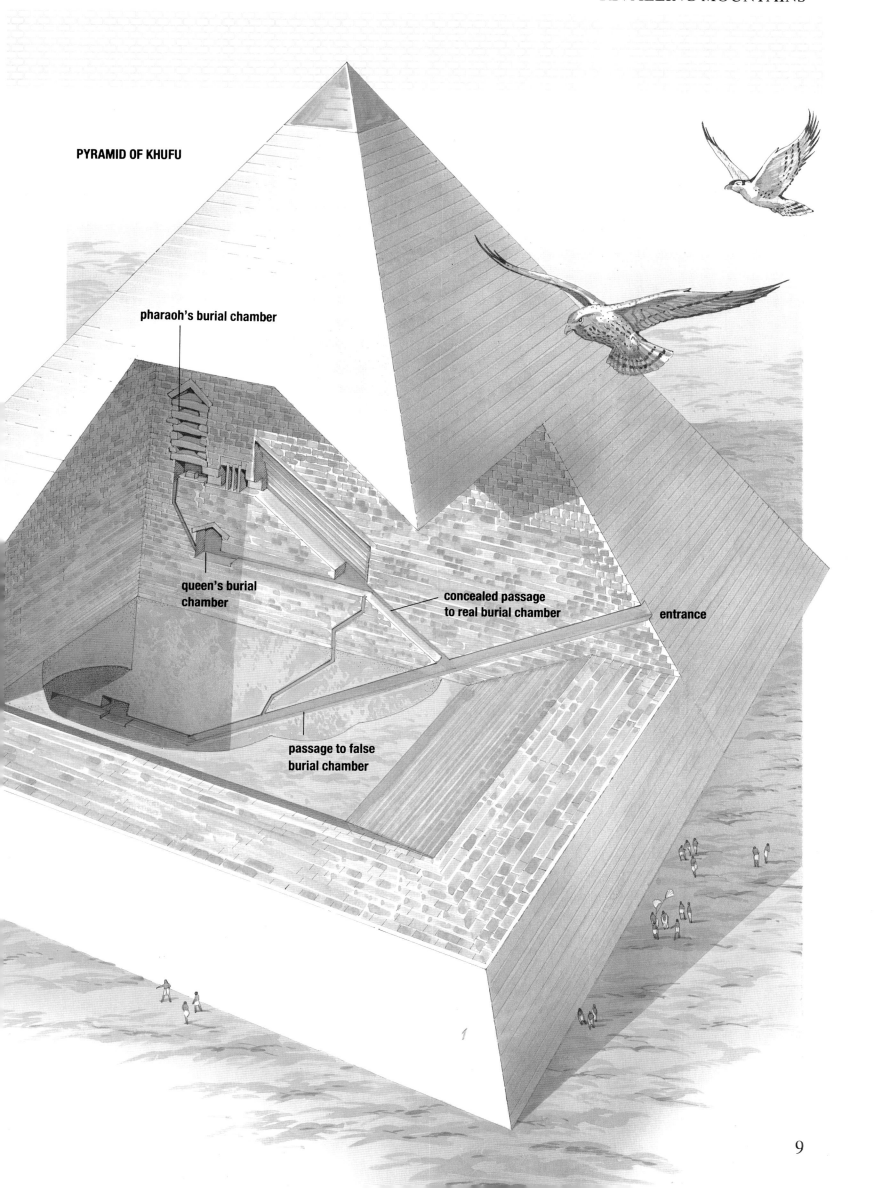

PYRAMID OF KHUFU

pharaoh's burial chamber

queen's burial chamber

concealed passage to real burial chamber

entrance

passage to false burial chamber

SEVEN GREAT WONDERS

The Egyptian master-builder Imhotep made the first Pyramid for his Pharaoh, Zoser, at Sakkara in 2778 B.C. It was later dwarfed by the Great Pyramids of Giza – the only one of the Seven Wonders of the Ancient World still to be seen. Each pyramid is made up of two million blocks of stone, weighing about 5 million tonnes. Khufu's Pyramid, the biggest of them all, was originally 147 m high (it is now 137 m).

The other six Wonders were much smaller than the Great Pyramids. But each, built between 600 and 270 B.C., was a spectacular achievement of engineering and art for its time.

THE SIX VANISHED WONDERS
The Seven Wonders passed into legend. Pictures of the six vanished structures were made, based on travellers' accounts and, in the case of two of the Wonders – the superb Temple of Artemis at Ephesus and Mausoleum at Halicarnassus – on the marble fragments that remain of these once richly decorated buildings.

Two of the Wonders were figures: the ivory and gold Statue of Zeus at Olympia and the Colossus of Rhodes, a giant statue beside the city's harbour mouth. Another, the Hanging Gardens of Babylon, probably decorated the brick terraces of an artificial mountain, such as a ziggurat, a kind of stepped pyramid. Only one of the Seven was built to be useful. This was the Pharos, or Lighthouse, of Alexandria in North Africa. At its top, 122 m high, a fire fuelled by toiling slaves shone for centuries as a beacon to ships.

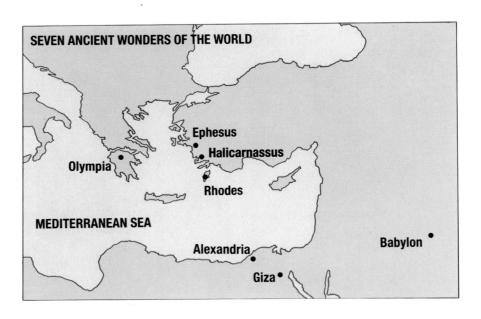

SEVEN ANCIENT WONDERS OF THE WORLD

Ephesus
Halicarnassus
Olympia
Rhodes
MEDITERRANEAN SEA
Babylon
Alexandria
Giza

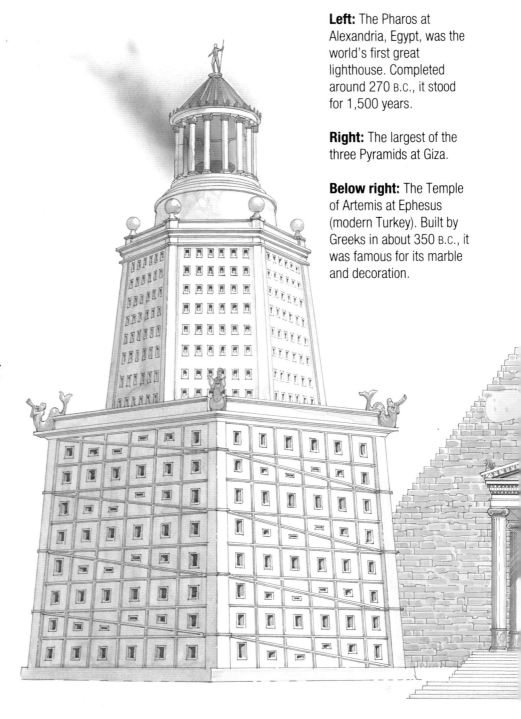

Left: The Pharos at Alexandria, Egypt, was the world's first great lighthouse. Completed around 270 B.C., it stood for 1,500 years.

Right: The largest of the three Pyramids at Giza.

Below right: The Temple of Artemis at Ephesus (modern Turkey). Built by Greeks in about 350 B.C., it was famous for its marble and decoration.

Below: The statue of Zeus at Olympia, Greece, was made in the 5th century B.C. and stood 12 m high.

Right: The Hanging Gardens of Babylon (modern Iraq), built in about 600 B.C. by King Nebuchadnezzar.

Below centre: As tall as the Statue of Liberty, the Colossus of Rhodes stood beside the harbour entrance from 280 to 224 B.C.

Below right: The tomb of King Mausolus at Halicarnassus (modern Turkey) was built in about 325 B.C.

SACRIFICIAL MOUNTAINS

Across the other side of the world from the Egyptians, civilizations in the Americas also built great pyramids. These were the Maya, Toltec, and Aztec peoples. Their cities are empty now, some overgrown by thick jungle, and their stone roads have long since crumbled.

At Teotihuacan, in Mexico, the Pyramid of the Sun was built before A.D. 700. Its five tiers rise 60 m from a base of over 600 m long. At the top stood a temple, from where the priests looked down onto the worshipping crowds below.

Below: In Central America, temple priests discuss preparations for another sacrificial victim. Huge crowds below witnessed these bloody rituals, believing that each death helped to ensure the continuance of the world. A ceremonial way, "the road of the dead", led to the pyramid. On top, the hearts of the victims were cut out and held up still beating.

Many of the New World pyramids were used for bloody human sacrifices. When the great temple at Tenochtitlan, capital of the Aztecs, was dedicated in 1487, 20,000 victims were slaughtered. Temple priests cut off the victims' heads and flung the corpses down the stone steps.

The builders of these huge structures worked without wheels, iron tools, or horses to haul loads. The pyramid design was simple, perhaps based on the village hut, which today still has an earth platform above a short stairway.

Similarities between the American pyramids and the ziggurats of ancient Babylon led some people to think that builders from the Old World might have sailed to the New long before Columbus in 1492.

America's sacrificial temples were abandoned soon after the Spanish conquistadors arrived in 1519. Tenochtitlan was taken and sacked. The Spaniards brought Christianity, the horse, and the sword. Within a few years, the culture that built the pyramids of America was no more.

Above and Below: The Pyramid of the Sun at Teotihuacan is surrounded by smaller pyramids. Teotihuacan was an important religious and trade centre in Mexico, about the same time as the Maya civilization (200 B.C. to A.D. 700). The people who built it remain unknown, as does the reason for its end.

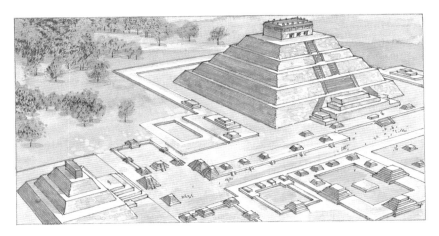

BUILDINGS FOR GODS

Religion has been the great inspiration for buildings all over the world. Some of the more remarkable ones include the Egyptian Temple of Isis at Philae, the Temple of Amon at Karnak, the cave temples in India at Ajanta and Ellora, the Buddhist temples at Angkor Wat in Cambodia, and the Parthenon in Greece.

THE PARTHENON
Athens is today a bustling and polluted capital city, but above the noise of the busy streets stands a serene ruin – the Parthenon. High on top of the Acropolis hill, within sight of the gods on Mount Olympus, it is surely one of the most beautiful and deservedly famous of architectural wonders.

The Parthenon was constructed between 447 and 432 B.C., when Athens was at the peak of its power, to house a statue of the city's goddess, Athena Parthenos. For a thousand or more years before, Cretans and Myceneans had built similar temples, but nothing as magnificent as the Parthenon. This was a wooden building re-created in stone. Its dimensions were worked out mathematically to precise ratios and it was lavishly decorated.

As Greece's grandeur faded, the Parthenon was taken over by other religions. It became a Christian church, an Islamic mosque, and, finally, even a gunpowder store. By the nineteenth century, it was in ruins. Some of its sculptures were removed by Lord Elgin to the British Museum in London. Today air pollution has damaged the stone, but a major restoration programme is under way.

Left: The Egyptian temples at Philae and Karnak were dedicated to individual gods. Beyond the pylons, or gate-towers, a series of spaces became smaller and darker approaching the innermost sanctuary.

Above: The marble used to build the Parthenon came from Mount Pentelicus near Athens. The building measures 72 m by 34 m, and its roof was originally 18 m high. Tilts and curves were built in to correct optical illusions. Straight columns would have made the building look narrower in the middle.

Right: The white-domed Bodnath temple, a famous Buddhist shrine in Kathmandu, Nepal. The Indian style of the carved stone stupa contrasts with the Chinese–Tibetan style of the pagoda, with its painted eyes and fluttering prayer flags.

MOUNDS AND CIRCLES

People with no apparent skill in building with wood or stone still left huge monuments. They piled up mounds of earth so enormous as to be mistaken for hills in the landscape. Monk's Mound in Illinois, USA, is 30 m high with a bigger base than that of the Great Pyramid. It was made by the Mississippians, native American city-builders, whose culture lasted from about A.D. 700 until the 1700s.

To move hundreds of tonnes of soil by muscle power alone took great organization. The scale of the Great Serpent Mound in Ohio is best seen from above. It looks like a giant snake 400 m long.

Below: Stonehenge as it is today. Originally, there were two circles and two inner horseshoes of stones within an earth ditch. Pairs of stones were capped by massive lintels.

Below: Great Serpent Mound was built by the Adena peoples of western North America in about 100 B.C. The mound may have been built as a sacred image.

Right: In pre-Roman Britain people cut figures into chalk hillsides. Some show "long men" (human figures), such as the Cerne Abbas Giant in Dorset. There are also 17 chalk horses, like this one in Wiltshire.

In Europe too, people raised giant mounds, usually as burial sites. There are 30,000 barrows, or burial-mounds, in England alone, including the biggest in Europe, at Silbury Hill in Wiltshire. This stands 40 m high and has a ditch 6 m deep all around it. It was built about 4,700 years ago, but why is a mystery. No human remains have been found inside it. All we know is that its builders shifted 680,000 tonnes of chalk by hand to make it.

As well as mounds, standing stones, with names such as Long Meg or Devil's Den, were also set up in ancient Europe. The stones mark a grave or some sacred or religious site. The most famous of all the prehistoric monuments of this type is Stonehenge. Built in stages from about 2800 B.C., this complex of gigantic stone blocks arranged in a circle stands on Salisbury Plain in England. To drag each stone, some of them weighing almost 50 tonnes, and put it in place, would have needed 500 men. According to some legends, Stonehenge could only have been built by the Devil.

HOMES

Right: The builders of the town houses of Çatal Hüyük (today part of Turkey) were worried about being attacked. The mud-brick houses were built close together to form a defensive barrier. Whether the settlement was also surrounded by a protective wall is not known. Çatal Hüyük was one of the earliest towns, dating back to at least 6000 B.C. About 5,000 people lived in the town, which had about 1,000 houses, each occupying some 25 sq m.

Above: Cliff-face dwellings provided protection from enemies and the weather. These extraordinary homes, rather like human birds' nests, were made by people in Cappadoccia, now part of modern Turkey. Whole villages including some 600 churches were carved into the rock during the tenth and eleventh centuries. Some of the churches are famous for the frescoes painted on the cave walls. The area is also known for its remarkable rock formations that occurred naturally from the erosion of the softer rock layers.

Left: The cliff villages of Mesa Verde, in Colorado, USA, were rediscovered in the 1880s, having been abandoned for 500 years. The houses were well-preserved, as were the villagers' possessions, which were covered in dust. Some of the rooms, which had probably once been apartments, had been set aside for storing belongings. The biggest dwelling, Cliff Palace, is believed to have been inhabited by about 400 people and to have served as a regional centre for other villages of Mesa Verde.

The first cities were in the Near East, where the climate was hot. Homes had small doors and windows and stood close together to shade the walls. In Persia (modern Iran) and India, wind-catchers – openings on the roof – let in cooling air.

As long ago as 5500 B.C., people were city-dwellers in places such as Khirokitia, a collection of 1,000 domed houses on the island of Cyprus. By 2500 B.C. the city of Mohenjo Daro (in modern Pakistan) had 40,000 inhabitants. Its remains include large houses, with several courtyards surrounded by rooms. All the houses had a well and a bathroom, with brick drainpipes taking dirty water away to covered drains in the street.

In cooler climates, houses were built with central heating, such as the hypocaust hot-air system of the Romans. The Romans also developed high-rise living. Their city-planners designed tenement blocks of brick and concrete, with wooden floors. Often these were six or seven storeys high.

CLIFF-DWELLERS

At Mesa Verde in the American South-West, people made their homes by hollowing out the sides of a canyon cut by the Mancos River. The homes – some multi-storeyed – are built into sheer sandstone cliffs.

The biggest dwelling, the Cliff Palace, has 200 apartment-rooms and in places is four storeys high. It includes underground rooms, or *kivas*, where the Indians held religious ceremonies. Although the climate was dry and people's homes were draughty, at least the hillside villages were safe from attack.

ARENAS AND THEATRES

At the bustling centre of the city of modern Rome stands a traffic island – the 2,000-year-old Colosseum, which was once Ancient Rome's greatest stadium.

Today the Colosseum is an empty shell of brick tiers and arches. The arena floor, where gladiators used to fight each other to the death, has rotted to dust. Beneath it are the storerooms, and the cages where wild animals, captured for the entertainment of the bloodthirsty crowd, were once penned-up.

The Colosseum was huge, measuring 48 m high, 189 m long, and 55 m wide. Spectators sat on rows and rows of wood and stone benches. The patricians – the rich and famous – were at the front, the plebeians – common people – occupied the topmost tiers. The Colosseum opened in A.D. 80 with a 100-day-long festival of gladiator contests, fights between men and wild animals, and a mock naval battle for which the arena was flooded. For over 300 years the Colosseum hosted such spectacles.

Above: The Colosseum was the largest amphitheatre in the Roman Empire. Its crowd capacity was 87,000.

Right: Fights between gladiators were popular attractions in the Colosseum. Some gladiators fought with swords and daggers, others with a long net and a trident. There were also gladiators on horseback and in chariots. Gladiators were trained in combat schools, and were sworn to fight to the death. A defeated gladiator might be shown mercy if he had fought well. The crowd waved their handkerchiefs to show that they wanted his life to be spared.

Above: The theatre at Epidaurus has superb acoustics. A person speaking from the orchestra, or stage, can be clearly heard all around the bowl-shaped seating area.

By the seventh century the Colosseum was abandoned. It had been a theatre of cruelty. The theatres built earlier by the Greeks were far more civilized. In Greece, birthplace of Western drama, the first audiences sat or stood on a sloping hillside to watch the performance below. Later, rows of seats were cut in a semicircle around the flat "stage". The beautiful theatre at Epidaurus was designed by the architect Polyclitus around 340 B.C. Almost every seat remains in place and plays are still performed there.

GREAT WALLS

The Great Wall of China is the longest structure ever built. It stretches 2,400 km, west from the Yellow Sea to the Jade Gate, where the ancient Silk Road winds its way into the vast emptiness of Central Asia.

The wall was begun in 214 B.C. by order of Shih Huang Ti, the first emperor of all China, to keep out barbarian raiders. Separate border walls that already existed were strengthened and joined together to form a continuous winding fortification. Much of the basic wall is a stone rampart 9 m high, with a road along the top. Every 60 m or so there is a watch tower 12 m high, from where guards lit fires to send signals along the wall. Elsewhere, the wall is just an earth bank.

The building of the Great Wall was an enormous task. Most of those who worked on it were convicts, of whom perhaps a million died in its construction.

ROMAN WALLS

A smaller wall was built by the Romans to protect the northern frontier of Britain. About 6 m high, the mostly stone and turf wall ran 118 km from Wallsend on the River Tyne in the east to Bowness on Solway in the west.

Work was completed in A.D. 136, on orders of the Emperor Hadrian. The wall itself was easily torn down by marauding tribes from Scotland. But the stone forts along its length, garrisoned by the Roman Army, served as effective frontier posts. To this extent the wall seems to have fulfilled its purpose until 383, when the Romans pulled back southwards, leaving the wall as a monument to Roman occupation.

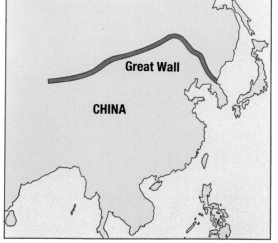

The Chinese Great Wall, made up of stone walls and earthworks, and with branches at various points, may once have been 9,000 km long.

Above: The Great Wall of China was built to guard against attacks by Turkish and Mongol tribesmen in the third century B.C. The Chinese call it "the longest graveyard in the world" because of the many thousands of workers who died in the building of it.

Right: View of Hadrian's Wall near Housesteads. Housesteads is the best-preserved of the 16 garrison forts along the wall. Smaller forts, or "milecastles", were built at intervals of 1,481 m (a Roman mile).

SCOTLAND

Hadrian's Wall

ENGLAND

LOST WORLDS

Why did an ancient people trace lines in desert earth, making pictures so huge they can be seen clearly only from the air? This is the mystery of the Nazca lines of Peru. These giant patterns of birds, snakes, and other creatures were made by the Nazca people many hundreds of years before aircraft flew in the skies. Perhaps they meant their pictures to be seen by the gods.

The Nazca civilization has vanished, like others of South America. But evidence of some lost civilizations has re-emerged in the jungles and the hills. Over 2,700 m high in the Andes Mountains of Peru lie the ruins of Machu Picchu, lost city of the Incas. Built in the 1400s, the terraced city was abandoned when the Spaniards crushed the Inca Empire in the 1500s, and was not rediscovered until 1911. The buildings include stone houses, burial caves, a royal palace, and a military barracks.

STONE CITY IN AFRICA

The ruins that stand on a high plateau between the Zambezi and Limpopo Rivers in modern Zimbabwe once belonged to the old city of Great Zimbabwe. It was the sight of these stone walls that excited the imagination of European explorers to Africa with tales of lost treasure and legends of the ancient Queen of Sheba.

Zimbabwe's mysterious walls hid no gold, but in themselves are an impressive achievement. The biggest buildings were made by the Shona people up to 900 years ago. They include a tower 9 m high and walls over 240 m long, made of granite slabs fitted together without mortar. The Rozwi people later took over the city, adding more stonework, but in the 1800s Great Zimbabwe was abandoned.

Right: Machu Picchu was built 2,700 m up in the Andes Mountains. It has sheer 600-m cliffs on three sides and a moat and stone walls on the fourth. The Incas grew crops on fields cut into the mountainside.

These ruins in south-central Zimbabwe date from 1100 to 1500 A.D. They are probably the remains of the palace of the kings of the Shona people who lived in this part of Africa.

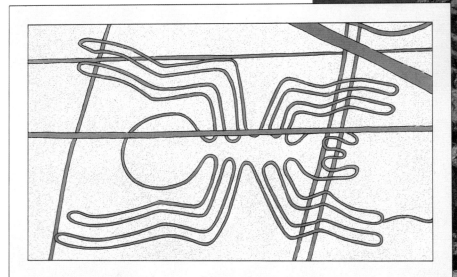

The Nazca people of Peru, dating from about 370 B.C. to A.D. 450, created giant shapes in the landscape, like this spider and lines, perhaps to follow the movement of the Sun in the sky.

ARCHES AND AQUEDUCTS

F ive thousand years ago a building technique was discovered that made new shapes and designs possible for big buildings. This discovery was the arch, which gives great strength and can span wide spaces.

Before the arch, the roof of a big building had beams resting on side walls or columns. Any roof over 7 m wide was dangerous, as the beams were likely to bend and snap. The arch and the vault (a development of the arch) enabled Roman architects to build bigger and higher than ever before.

Right and Below: The arch is made by fitting together a series of stone wedges, called voussoirs. The keystone, at the top, is the last to be put in place. The Arch of Constantine (below) was built in Rome to celebrate the victory of the Emperor Constantine over his rebellious rival Maxentius in A.D. 312.

The first arches were simple: just three or four stones fitted together. The Romans explored the range of possibilities to the utmost. They built triumphal arches. They laid arches side by side and on top of one another. They built arched complexes, such as the Baths of Caracalla, where 1,600 bathers could enjoy hot and cold pools beneath a domed roof. Concrete arches supported the Colosseum and other amphitheatres. In the Pantheon, the Romans perfected the dome. The huge interior is 43 m wide, with an opening in the crown of the dome to let in daylight.

Below: The Baths of Caracalla in Rome were built in the early 3rd century A.D. They included this swimming pool, hot and cold rooms, and dressing rooms. Around the bath complex were meeting rooms and a stadium.

THE AQUEDUCT

Many Mediterranean towns had problems with water supply. To bring water to thirsty citizens, the Romans built aqueducts. These water-carrying bridges arched across valleys, carrying as much as 30 million litres of water a day. The most spectacular is the Pont du Gard, built in A.D. 19 near Nîmes in France. Its three tiers rise impressively to a height of 48 m.

Below: The Roman aqueduct at Segovia, known as El Puente, was constructed during the reign of the Emperor Trajan (A.D. 53–117). It is 900 m long and 30 m high, and it still carries water today.

MONUMENTS AND MYSTERIES

Easter Island
Easter Island (right) is extremely isolated. It is midway between South America and the nearest Pacific islands to the west. Statues (below) can be seen at Rano Raraku, the quarry where the Easter Island statues, or *moai*, were made. The islanders carved the face first, before cutting the whole statue from the rock.

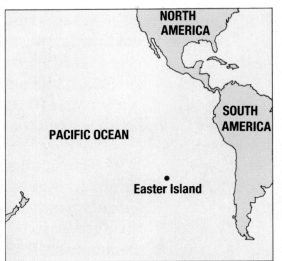

NORTH AMERICA

PACIFIC OCEAN

SOUTH AMERICA

Easter Island

How did the 50-tonne statues on Easter Island get where they are? This was the puzzle that the Norwegian anthropologist Thor Heyerdahl set out to solve.

The statues once had eyes. So do similar figures in Mexico, and also the heads made by the Ancient Hittite people of the Near East. Could there be a link between Old and New Worlds?

Easter Island in the eastern Pacific is famous for its mysterious stone statues. There are about 600 of them, and more left unfinished. When Europeans discovered the island in 1722, many statues were still standing, but were later toppled. They had been made between A.D. 900 and 1600 by islanders known as "Long Ears", who sailed to Easter Island from South America.

The stone giants were moved, Heyerdahl discovered, but not across continents. Tests showed how the statues were originally dragged upright from the island quarry on ropes.

COLOSSI AND NEEDLES

The Colossi of Memnon are statues of the Egyptian king Amenhotep III (1417–1379 B.C.). Today the two giant royal figures sit forlornly on Egyptian farmland, the last link with the temple that Amenhotep built at Thebes.

To mark important events, the Egyptians put up obelisks – granite pillars engraved with hieroglyphs (Egyptian writing). Some obelisks weigh over 200 tonnes. The Romans carried off several obelisks to Rome. In the 1800s two more, known as Cleopatra's Needles, were brought to London and New York, where they still stand.

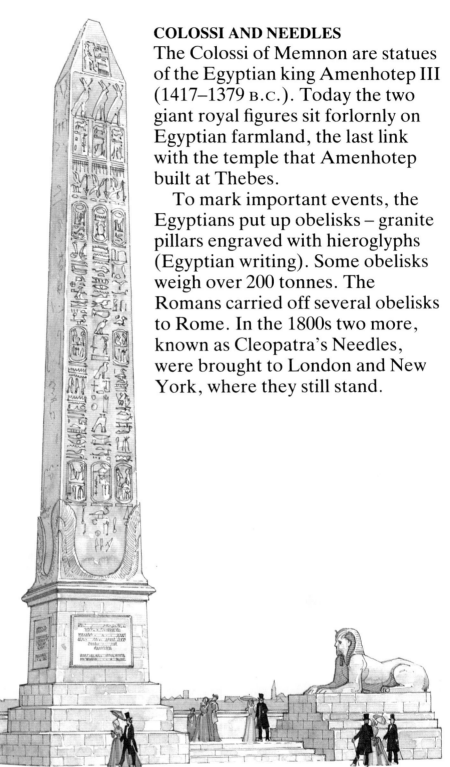

EGYPTIAN GIANTS
The Colossi of Memnon at Thebes, now weathered and cracked by time, were once nearly 21 m high. Each statue was cut from a single block of stone.

Above and Left:
Cleopatra's Needle was shipped from Egypt to London in 1877 in a cigar-shaped barge. When it seemed that the barge was about to sink, it was left to drift for five days off the coast of Spain. Then it was recovered and towed into London. Cleopatra's Needle now stands beside the River Thames.

CASTLES

Hilltop forts were built as long ago as the Stone Age. The Romans were great fort-builders, as were the Byzantines, who established the Eastern Roman Empire and built castles in North Africa about 1,500 years ago. The great age of Western castles began in the Middle Ages about the year 1000. The Normans built castles in England, the Moors in Spain, and the Crusaders in the Holy Land (Palestine).

Below: Medieval Crusaders attacking a castle in the Holy Land. Siege machines – such as giant catapults and slings – were used to batter the castle walls with heavy missiles or hurl missiles over the walls to reach the enemy sheltering within.

Right: Neuschwanstein Castle in Bavaria, Germany, was built in the late 1800s for King Ludwig II of Bavaria. Looking like a Walt Disney fantasy castle, it is an accurate reproduction of the type found in Germany during the Middle Ages.

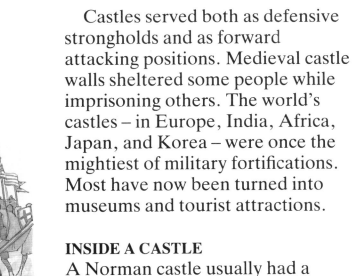

Castles served both as defensive strongholds and as forward attacking positions. Medieval castle walls sheltered some people while imprisoning others. The world's castles – in Europe, India, Africa, Japan, and Korea – were once the mightiest of military fortifications. Most have now been turned into museums and tourist attractions.

INSIDE A CASTLE

A Norman castle usually had a central tower, called a keep. The castle's stone walls enclosed baileys (courtyards). From the walls, soldiers could shoot at the enemy below and drop boiling oil and large boulders on them.

The concentric castle, which had circular walls within walls, was an Eastern design copied in Europe. If one wall fell, the defenders fell back behind the next. To capture the castle, the attackers had to smash down gates, scramble across bridges, and avoid dead-end traps, which exposed them to cross-fire. The defenders could make raids on the enemy from gates called salley-ports. A castle on the scale of Krak des Chevaliers in Syria, the biggest Crusader castle, could resist a siege lasting a whole year.

CATHEDRALS

The builders of medieval cathedrals looked skywards. They were building to the glory of God. In their efforts to go higher and higher they sought to defy gravity and build tall structures on only shallow foundations.

But there were major disasters. Towers collapsed under their own weight (Beauvais, France), or fell in storms (Lincoln, England) or were struck by lightning (Old St. Paul's, London).

To support the enormous weight of stonework, the medieval builders invented flying buttresses. These were ribs of stone that arched out and away from the walls to carry the strain to the ground.

The walls, freed by the buttresses from load-bearing, became picture frames for windows. Daylight streamed into the cathedral through panels of coloured glass.

Chartres Cathedral in France has some of the finest windows as well as 10,000 magnificent statues. It took just 27 years to build, after the old church burned down in 1194.

THE WORLD'S GREATEST
Milan Cathedral in Italy, built between 1386 and 1485, is the second-largest medieval cathedral after Seville in Spain. Outside it is an intricate maze of buttresses and pinnacles; inside, beneath the 45-m high vault, it is cool and shady.

Huge cathedrals are still being built today. The Cathedral of St. John the Divine in New York is unfinished after 100 years. Its nave, measuring 181 m, is the longest in the world. In the Côte d'Ivoire in West Africa there is a new basilica whose size is second only to St. Peter's in Rome.

Above: The front of Chartres Cathedral in France. The left-hand spire, begun in 1134 but not completed until the 1500s, is the taller of the two, at 113 m. The shorter spire was built between 1145 and 1165. Between 1200 and 1236, 175 stained-glass windows for the cathedral were made by master glaziers.

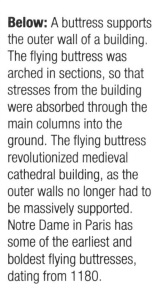

Right: Milan Cathedral is the most impressive Gothic cathedral in Italy. It has over 2,000 statues and 135 pinnacles. On the highest pinnacle stands a gold-covered figure of the Virgin Mary. The cathedral (the third on its site) was begun in the 1400s but was still being added to as recently as the 1950s.

Below: A buttress supports the outer wall of a building. The flying buttress was arched in sections, so that stresses from the building were absorbed through the main columns into the ground. The flying buttress revolutionized medieval cathedral building, as the outer walls no longer had to be massively supported. Notre Dame in Paris has some of the earliest and boldest flying buttresses, dating from 1180.

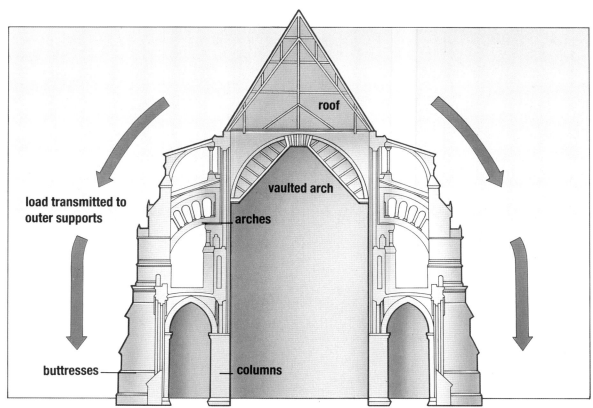

load transmitted to outer supports

roof

vaulted arch

arches

buttresses

columns

TOWERS AND SPIRES

The problem with tall towers is that they need support – a fact that the builders of the Leaning Tower of Pisa soon found out. The Italian city's *campanile* (bell-tower) was begun in 1154. But only three out of eight storeys were finished before the tilt became obvious. The soft damp clay on which the tower rested could not support it. Its builders tried to compensate by making the topmost stonework taller on the sinking side. This made the tower slightly banana-shaped, and the extra weight merely made it sink more.

The 56-m high Leaning Tower was finished in the 1300s. The stops and starts on its construction – caused by money problems as well as engineers' doubts – saved it. The pauses allowed the tower to settle. Otherwise, it might have collapsed.

Galileo's experiments
The great scientist Galileo Galilei (1564–1642) was born in Pisa and taught mathematics there. In 1590 he supposedly dropped a large and a small cannon ball from the top of the Leaning Tower. Both hit the ground at almost the same moment. Galileo concluded that all falling objects accelerate at the same rate.

Below: The Chinese pagoda has a regular design: each storey is the same shape (round, square, or many-sided) but smaller than the one below it. The pagoda represents earth and heaven. The storeys are like terraces cut into a mountain slope. The discs on the rooftop represent the heavens.

In the future, Pisa's tower could still topple. It leans a little more each year. At present it is braced with steel cables until engineers work out a permanent way to prop it up. It was from the Tower of Pisa that Galileo is supposed to have carried out his famous experiments on the behaviour of falling objects.

TOWERING PAGODAS

A pagoda is a temple of the Buddhist religion. Through the heart of the pagoda runs a mast or pillar, symbolizing the union of heaven and earth.

The Chinese developed their pagodas from lookout towers built 3,000 years ago. China's oldest pagoda was built in 523 and is 27 m high. The tallest pagoda – 115 m – is the nineteenth-century Phra Pathom Chedi pagoda in Thailand.

MOSQUES AND TEMPLES

The first Islamic mosques were modelled on the courtyard of the home of the most holy Prophet Muhammad in Medina (Saudi Arabia). Around the central space are four halls, or *iwans*. On one inner wall is the *mihrab*, an arch or niche to show the direction of Mecca, the holy city which Muslims kneel to face when at prayer.

The great mosques of the world are jewels of Islamic art. Domes gleam in the sunlight. Glazed blue tiles sparkle. Green lawns and fountains greet visiting pilgrims.

When the Turks captured Constantinople in 1453, they converted the Byzantine Christian church of Hagia Sophia into a mosque. Hagia Sophia was built for the Emperor Justinian in A.D. 537 in just six years. Its dome measures over 30 m in diameter and 50 m high. Light from the base of the dome hides its supports, so the vast bowl seems to float, "as if suspended on a cord from heaven".

TEMPLE IN THE JUNGLE

In the 1860s a French traveller to the jungles of Cambodia spotted stone towers above the treetops. He had rediscovered the lost capital of the Khmer Empire, abandoned since the 1400s.

Its most amazing structure is the temple of Angkor Wat, the biggest religious building in the world. It was built in honour of the Hindu god Vishnu between A.D. 1113 and 1150 by King Suryavarman II.

Forgotten for 500 years, Angkor Wat is again being reclaimed by jungle. Cambodia, having suffered more than 20 years of war, has few resources with which to maintain so large an ancient monument.

Below and Right: The Hagia Sophia in modern Istanbul (Turkey). This magnificent Byzantine building has been both a Christian church and an Islamic mosque. It is now a museum that attracts overseas tourists.

Below: The temple complex of Angkor Wat is within a moated enclosure measuring 1,555 m by 1,370 m. At its heart are five towers, the tallest almost 70 m high.

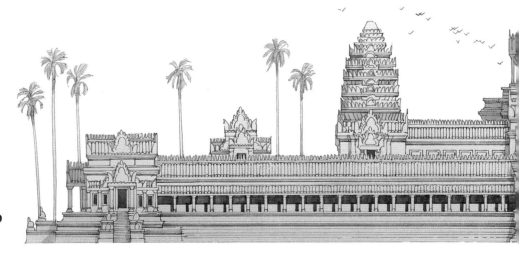

Above: This golden-domed shrine of Fatimah is at Qom in Iran. Its style is typical of classic Islamic architecture. An Islamic mosque can be a simple hall, or a rich and beautiful building.

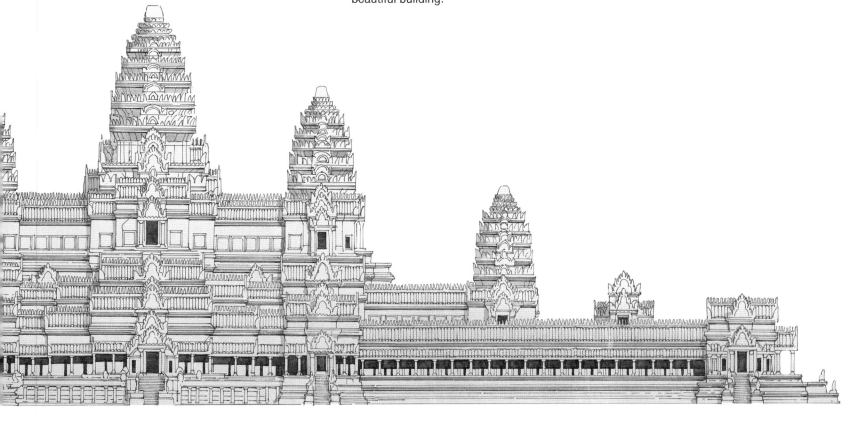

FORBIDDEN CITIES

Mecca is the holiest of Muslim cities. Every devout Muslim hopes to visit Mecca as a pilgrim. At Mecca's heart is the Ka'bah, a cube-shaped building said to have been built by Abraham. In about A.D. 570 the Prophet Muhammad was born in Mecca. Muhammad banished the idols of pagan religion from the city, and dedicated Mecca to Allah, the one true god.

In 1853 the British explorer Sir Richard Burton journeyed to Mecca, disguised as a pilgrim. Today Muslims from all over the world mingle in the city during the *hajj* (pilgrimage). Non-Muslims are not permitted to enter Mecca.

BEIJING'S HIDDEN WORLD

The Mongol emperors built on a scale never seen before in China. In Beijing they created the Imperial Palace, a city within a city, and the heart of China's government. Only the Emperor and his family could enter the innermost part, the Forbidden City.

Work on the city, which covered 1000 m by 750 m, began in 1406. Beyond the Wu Min Gate were five bridges over the moat. Across the moat, steps led to a courtyard surrounded by three vast halls, and beyond them lay the imperial living quarters and three palaces, each with its own gardens.

The Communist rulers of modern China guard another forbidden city: Lhasa in Tibet. Its monasteries and the Potola Palace, home of the Buddhists' holy leader the Dalai Lama, stand on a plain 3,600 m above sea level. For centuries mountains and deserts barred the way to Lhasa. Today it is China's rulers who bar the way.

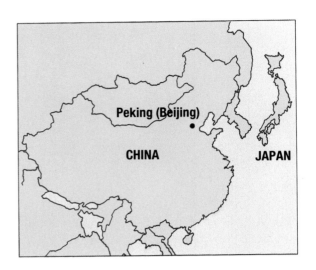

Below: Like most Chinese public buildings built between about 1100 and 1500 A.D., those of the Imperial Palace in Beijing (formerly called Peking) were made of wood on a stone foundation and had tiled roofs with upturned edges. The roofs were supported by wooden columns. The wood was stained or painted bright colours.

Right: Carved lions guard the approach to the Tai-ho-Tien, or Hall of Great Peace, China. Built in the late 1600s, this is the biggest of three great halls within Beijing's Imperial Palace. In China, such buildings were based on a traditional plan, and in accordance with ancient religious ideas.

EUROPEAN SPLENDOURS

The Renaissance – the rebirth of art and learning in Europe – began in the late 1300s in Italy. Renaissance architects and artists, inspired by mathematics, became fascinated by perspective, form, and decoration.

THE CITY ON THE SEA

Venice is a city of light, colour, and water. Once the island home of poor fishermen, by the 1200s it had become rich through trade with the East. Today its glorious buildings are in danger of sinking beneath the waters of the Adriatic Sea. At the heart of Venice, beside the Grand Canal, is St. Mark's Square, with its "golden church", which contains fine marble and carvings. The Palace of the Doge (Duke) was completed in the early 1400s.

ROME REBORN

St. Peter's Square in Rome was created in the seventeenth century by Gian Lorenzo Bernini. It forms a vast oval bounded by columns. In its centre is an Egyptian obelisk.

The great church of St. Peter's was built mostly in the 1500s. The dome, designed by Michelangelo, rests on four huge piers. A spiral staircase between the inner and outer shells of the dome leads up to the crown, and a fine panoramic view of the city.

In the Sistine Chapel, built in 1473, Michelangelo covered the ceiling with paintings. It took him four years (1508–1512). Later, on the altar wall, he created the fresco *The Last Judgement*, a single painting almost as large as the entire ceiling above.

Below: Venice at dusk, from the water. To the left is the campanile, or bell-tower, of St. Mark's Basilica. To the right is the Doge's Palace with its handsome arches.

Above: St. Peter's in Rome is the largest church in the world, with the biggest dome (42 m across). An Egyptian obelisk stands in the great open space in front of St. Peter's.

ROYAL POMP

A great age of royal building in Europe began in the early 1500s. Kings strove to outdo one another in the magnificence of their palaces such as Chambord, France (1519), and Hampton Court, England (1514). This extravagance contrasts with the Escorial Palace in Spain, built between 1563 and 1584 for the devout King Philip II.

Louis XIV of France was neither modest nor retiring. His Palace of Versailles, outside Paris, was begun in 1661. It was big enough to house his court of 20,000 people, and took 30,000 workers, with 6,000 pack-horses, to build. The interior was decorated with costly furnishings, and the grounds included a luxurious park and fine gardens. Louis and his successor also built two smaller palaces, the Grand and Petit Trianons, where the royal family could relax.

During the French Revolution of 1789, the Palace of Versailles was stripped of much of its finery. Now a museum, it has been restored to something like its original glory.

Above: The library of Spain's Escorial Palace contains some of the most valuable medieval books in the world. The huge building was a monastery as well as a royal palace.

THE TAJ MAHAL

In 1629 Mumtaz Mahal, favourite wife of the Mogul ruler of India, died in childbirth. The emperor Shah Jahan ordered for his wife the most beautiful tomb in the world.

Twenty thousand labourers and artists worked for 20 years to complete the Taj Mahal. Architects from all over the Muslim world offered advice. A Turk drew the final plans. The domed building is of white marble, resting on a red sandstone platform. At each corner is a minaret 40 m high. In the mausoleum itself Shah Jahan rests in peace beside his beloved wife.

Right: The Taj Mahal is often called the most beautiful building in the world. The quiet pool waters reflect perfect proportions: each of the building's four faces is identical. The dome rises almost 61 m above the floor, below which is the vault in which Shah Jahan and his wife are buried.

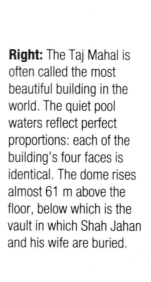

Right: The Palace of Versailles was once the centre of court life in France. Today its ornate rooms, halls, and gardens are a major attraction to the many tourists who visit Paris every year.

CANALS AND LOCKS

More than 2,000 years ago Greek seamen taking a short cut from the port of Piraeus to the Adriatic Sea had to drag their ships overland, across the Isthmus of Corinth. Today small ships can take the same route along the Corinth Canal, a waterway cut through the rock.

Canals were being built as long ago as 4000 B.C. The Chinese Grand Canal, 1700 km long, was dug in stages from 540 B.C. to A.D. 1327. It was probably the Chinese who, in about A.D. 900, invented the canal lock, which lets craft pass from one water level to another.

Right: A ship passing through the Corinth Canal. Work on cutting the 6-km long canal took 12 years (1881–1893). The canal is only 21 m wide so it is too narrow for large modern vessels.

GREECE
Athens
Corinth

Right: One of the 28 locks on the Caledonian Canal, which links the east and west coasts of Scotland. The canal connects a chain of lochs (lakes) and is almost 100 km long. It was built by Thomas Telford between 1803 and 1823, though work did not cease entirely until 1847.

From the 1400s, locks were in use on European canals, which carried most heavy goods before the coming of the railways in the 1800s. The use of the steam shovel and explosives in the nineteenth century enabled canals to be dug more quickly than ever before.

THE SUEZ CANAL

In 1859, work began on the Suez Canal, linking the Mediterranean and the Red Sea. Ten years later, digging was complete and the first ship steamed through.

The Suez Canal, which follows a chain of salt lakes left from a dried-up natural channel, is on one level, with no locks. Ships using it, on voyages between Europe and Asia, are saved a 7,000-km detour around Africa. Today, about 20,000 vessels pass through the Suez Canal and the Red Sea every year.

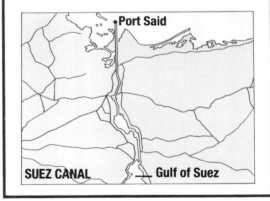

SUEZ CANAL
The Suez Canal is the largest big-ship canal in the world. It is deep enough for ships of 300,000 tonnes to steam the 162 km from Port Said to the Gulf of Suez.

Another great international waterway, the Panama Canal, links the Pacific and Atlantic Oceans. Opened in 1914, it is 80 km long and is used by about 13,000 ships annually. The St. Lawrence Seaway (1959) connects Atlantic Ocean-going shipping with the North American Great Lakes.

IRON MARVELS

When Gustave Eiffel announced plans to build a steel tower over 300 m high in Paris, many people thought he was mad. Some signed a petition of protest against such an outrage on the Paris skyline.

But the plan went ahead, and by March 1889 the tower, having taken just over two years to build, was ready for the Paris Exhibition. For 40 years the Eiffel Tower remained the world's tallest structure. It is made up of over 12,000 metal pieces, held together by more than 2 million metal rivets, and it weighs over 7,000 tonnes.

THE NEW IRON AGE

People have used iron tools and weapons for 5,000 years. But there were hardly any iron structures until the eighteenth century, when new processes for making iron and steel cheaply were developed during the Industrial Revolution. The first iron bridge was built at Coalbrookdale in England in 1779. In 1801 James Finley built the first iron-chain suspension bridge over Jacobs Creek in Pennsylvania, USA.

The first steel bridges followed in the 1870s. They included the Glasgow Bridge, opened in the USA in 1879, which spanned the Missouri River. The Forth Railway Bridge, built in Scotland between 1882 and 1890, was the first great steel cantilever bridge, with two main spans supported at their ends by towers. It was bigger than any earlier bridge and strong enough to withstand violent storms like the one which, in 1879, blew down the Tay railway bridge and claimed the lives of over 70 people.

Above: The Forth Bridge has twin 520-m spans. The three huge cantilevering towers are 100 m high and over 400 m long. The bridge's 58,000 tonnes of steelwork needs continuous repainting. The bridge remains extremely strong, more than a century after it was built.

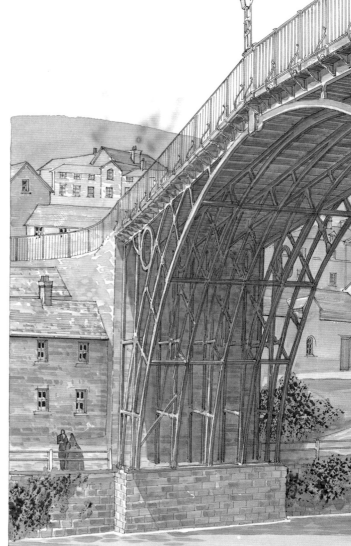

Right: The world's first iron bridge was built over the River Severn at Coalbrookdale in Shropshire, England. It was there that smelting of iron in a blast furnace was tried for the first time. The bridge's cast-iron beams were joined by carpenter's joints, as if they were wood. The bridge contains far more ironwork than is really needed.

Right: The Eiffel Tower is probably the best-known city landmark in the world. It was built for the 1889 Paris Exhibition to commemorate the 100th anniversary of the start of the French Revolution. The tower rose in stages, from June 1887 to March 1889. Such a remarkable rate of building was made possible by prefabricated steelwork being assembled on site.

BUILDINGS OF GLASS

The Crystal Palace was the wonder of London's Great Exhibition of 1851. Joseph Paxton sketched out a rough plan of the building on a sheet of blotting paper. Once given the go-ahead, he took just 10 days to work out the details and costs, down to the last nut and bolt.

Paxton had built glasshouses before, but never anything as large as the Crystal Palace. Assembled from mass-produced parts, it was 564 m long and 137 m broad. There were 84,000 sq m of sheet glass, 33,000 iron columns, 2,224 girders, and 55 km of rainwater gutters. At one time during the Exhibition, there were 93,000 visitors per day.

Afterwards, the Crystal Palace was dismantled and moved to a new site in London. It housed many events, from flower shows to concerts, until it burned to the ground in 1936.

Above: The Crystal Palace in London, England, as it looked soon after being built in the early 1850s. Of the immense structure of iron and glass, only the towers at each end were left standing following a great fire in 1936. The towers were pulled down in 1940.

Right: The Palm House at the Royal Botanic Gardens at Kew near London, was built by Decimus Burton in 1848. Burton worked with Joseph Paxton on several big glasshouses for English country homes.

Left: A sweeping arch of glass and steel forms the roof of Cologne railway station in Germany. Many large nineteenth-century railway stations had impressive roofs.

The sheet glass used for the Crystal Palace was a fairly new invention. Before the 1800s glass was very expensive, and made only in smallish pieces for windows and mirrors. With the coming of the Industrial Revolution, new glass-manufacturing processes enabled glass to be made cheaply, simply, and in large sheets.

BUILDINGS WITH GLASS

From then on, buildings could have not only big windows, but also roofs and walls made of glass. Railway stations were built with glass-panelled roofs to let in light, and from the 1850s, glass was used in pavements to admit light to cellars below. Unbreakable glass, with wire mesh inside, was invented in 1898. Using steel girders as a framework, architects could, if they wished, cover a whole building in glass.

MONUMENTS

Right: The granite cliff of Mount Rushmore rises some 2,000 m in the Black Hills of South Dakota. Sculptor Gutzon Borglum and his team worked from small-scale models as they drilled and blasted the four Presidential heads from the rock at the cliff face.

Today, near the Mount Rushmore National Memorial, work is going ahead on another rock sculpture. This will be a monument to the Sioux Indian chief Crazy Horse, and it will be 171 m high.

Four granite faces gaze from the side of Mount Rushmore in the Black Hills of South Dakota in the USA. They are the faces of four famous US Presidents: George Washington, Thomas Jefferson, Theodore Roosevelt, and Abraham Lincoln. Each of the heads is 18 m high. A complete statue on this scale would stand over 140 m tall.

The Mount Rushmore faces are a unique monument in stone. Workers began cutting away the mountain in 1927, using drills and dynamite. They worked from scale models of one-twelfth size made by the monument's designer, Gutzon Borglum. Borglum died shortly before the Mount Rushmore heads were finished in 1941.

The world's tallest statue is the 82-m high Motherland monument in Russia. This huge concrete figure was erected in 1967 in memory of those who died at the Battle of Stalingrad in World War II.

Probably the world's most famous statue is the Statue of Liberty. Standing on Liberty island in New York Harbour, it has given many immigrants their first sight of the New World.

Right: The Statue of Liberty is hollow inside. The tower-like iron frame is strong but flexible. It allows the statue's copper skin to react to wind and change of temperature without putting the supporting ironwork under stress.

Below: The face of Liberty is that of sculptor Auguste Bartholdi's mother. In the 1980s the statue was restored, and the old torch replaced with one closer to Bartholdi's original design.

The Statue of Liberty was designed by Auguste Bartholdi, a Frenchman. It was given to the USA by France in 1884 to commemorate US independence achieved 100 years earlier.

Beneath Liberty's flowing robes, made of 300 copper sheets, is a steel frame, which was designed by Gustave Eiffel. Inside is a spiral staircase with 142 steps. At the top, the observation platform in Liberty's crown can hold up to 20 people. Her glowing torch is 6.4 m high, and from toe to torch, the statue is 46 m tall.

MOUNTAIN TUNNELS

Building a tunnel is sometimes the only way to put a road or railway across a mountain. Often a tunnel also provides the shortest route, and it does not cause scarring of the landscape.

But tunnelling can be dangerous. On early tunnel projects, many workers were killed by explosions, rock falls, or flooding. The St. Gotthard rail tunnel, built between 1872 and 1881, killed 311 men and left 900 more so ill that they never worked again.

The first big mountain tunnels were built in the 1800s for the new railway networks across Europe and North America. In 1857, engineers working from both ends began cutting the Fréjus (Mont Cenis) tunnel to link France and Italy. This was the first great tunnel beneath the Alps. It was completed in 1871, and was the first tunnel dug by a boring machine that used compressed-air drills.

The St. Gotthard rail tunnel, also in the Alps, was the first major tunnel to be blasted with gelignite. The explosive was packed into holes bored by drills mounted on a platform called a jumbo. In the 1900s tunnel-boring was speeded up by fast, hard-tipped drills and the use of mechanized systems to carry away rubble.

The world's longest under-mountain road tunnels are all in Europe. Switzerland's St. Gotthard road tunnel, buit in 1980, is the record-holder, 16.32 km long. In second and third places are the Arlberg (Austria, 14 km) and the Fréjus (France–Italy, 13 km). The longest rail tunnel beneath mountains is the Simplon in the Alps, measuring 19.82 km.

Below: Building the St. Gotthard Tunnel (1872–1881). Much of the work was done by hand, in near-darkness and with poor ventilation.

Below: Section through a typical road tunnel, showing the entrances, roadway, and the giant concrete ventilation tubes constructed within the mountain rock.

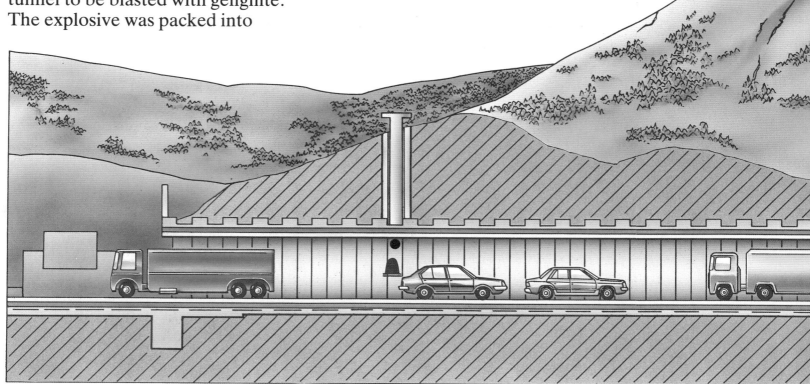

Right: Entrance to the Mont Blanc Tunnel on the Italian side of the Alps. Situated on the French–Italian frontier, it is the fourth-longest (11.7 km) of Europe's great mountain road tunnels.

RAILWAY CONSTRUCTION

The world's first public steam railway was the Stockton and Darlington Railway in north-east England, opened in 1825. It was followed, in 1830, by the Liverpool to Manchester line. For its 48 km of track, railway pioneers built a tunnel, a cutting 38 m deep, and more than 60 bridges.

The railway age was a period of hectic building which amazed the people of the time. Railway gangs blasted, dug, and hammered the iron rails across continents. The men who created the new transport system worked hard and lived rough. To cut costs, engineers avoided crossing rivers and mountains whenever possible. But if necessary, they boldly tunnelled through mountains and bridged rivers and gorges. In cities, stations became show-pieces of the new industrial age of the railways.

COAST-TO-COAST RAILS

In 1869, 38 years after the first US rail service began, two lines of tracks were joined at Promontory in Utah. The Union Pacific had started laying track westwards from Nebraska in 1865, two years after the Central Pacific set out eastwards from Sacramento, California. When the two lines met, the USA had its first coast-to-coast rail link. The railway helped to open up the West to settlers and unite the young American nation.

By 1885 Canada too had been crossed by rail, and by 1899 most of the 9,400-km track of the enormous Trans-Siberian Railway in Russia had been laid. The last stretch, around Lake Baikal, was complete by 1916 – making it the world's longest railway.

Above: With more than 3 billion passengers every year, Moscow has the world's most-used subway trains. Some of the stations are very elegant.

Below: Two steam locomotives at Sao Joao del Rei, Brazil. In most of South America, Africa and Asia, steam locomotives are still in regular use.

Above: Diesel locomotives and wagons of the Canadian Pacific (now CP Rail), one of the world's most spectacular railways. It covers a total distance of 4,600 km, from Montreal in the east to Vancouver in the west.

DAMS

Dams save water and produce power. A dam across a river creates an artificial lake called a reservoir. The stored water can be piped to crops, or through turbines to make electricity. The earliest dams, such as those in Jordan built over 5,000 years ago, were for crop irrigation. Huge modern dams, like the Aswan Dam in Egypt, which opened in 1970, provide water both for agriculture and for hydroelectric power.

TYPES OF DAM

Straight embankment dams made of soil and rock are ideal for wide shallow valleys. Embankment dams include the world's highest, such as the 310-m Nurek Dam in Russia and the 234-m Oroville Dam in the USA.

Curved or arch dams are stronger than straight dams. In 1589, Spaniards built the first arch dam, the Tibi Dam near Alicante. Until the 1800s it was the highest dam in the world. A concrete arch dam is the most suitable for a deep narrow valley. As water presses against the dam, the arch is squeezed more tightly against the valley sides. The world's first super-dam was the Hoover Dam (221 m high) on the Colorado River, USA, finished in 1936.

A gravity dam is a concrete wall whose sheer weight holds back the water. Grand Coulee Dam on the Columbia River, USA, is a concrete giant. Built in 1941, it is 167 m high, 1,272 m long, and contains 20 million tonnes of concrete.

Pipes called sluices channel water through a dam. The reservoir's water level is controlled by opening and closing valves.

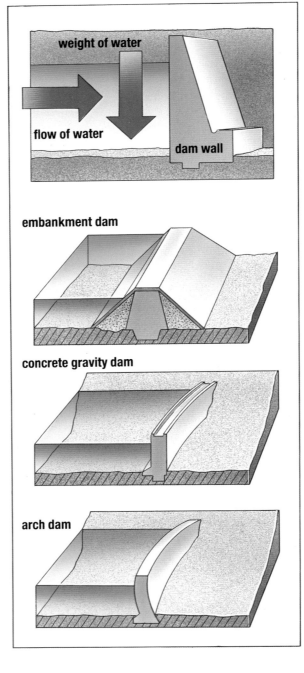

weight of water

flow of water

dam wall

embankment dam

concrete gravity dam

arch dam

Left: Embankment dams are made of earth and rock, dug from the site and heaped on top of a trench filled with clay or concrete, to stop water seeping through. An embankment dam does not need to be sited across a valley with firm sides. Concrete dams are either gravity dams (like giant bookends) or arches wedged against the sides of a steep valley. The energy of the water behind the dam can be usefully harnessed in a hydroelectric power station.

Right: The Hoover Dam supplies water and electricity to millions of Americans. Behind the dam is the artificial Lake Mead, 185 km long.

Below: Constructing the Itaipu Dam on the Parana River, between Brazil and Paraguay. It is one of the largest hydroelectric dams, delivering 12,700 MW of power.

PORTS AND BRIDGES

The curving bay of Rio de Janeiro in Brazil is a natural harbour. Many other ports are artificial, made by building breakwaters and jetties out to sea and by dredging deep channels for ships. The great port of Rotterdam in the Netherlands began with a dam built in the 1200s across the marshy Rotte river. Engineers created a port from the mud flats. Rotterdam's Europoort, begun in 1958, is now Europe's gateway for sea trade.

BRIDGES

People have been building bridges ever since they first laid logs across a stream or knotted ropes to cross a gorge. Until the 1800s most big bridges were made of stone. The use of hydraulic cement, which stays hard under water, and steel girders and cables changed the shape of bridges. These new technologies made possible the giant bridges of today.

There are four main bridge types: beam, arch, cantilever, and suspension. Suspension bridges are best for crossing wide rivers. They do not rest on piers built in the water, so there is more room for ships to pass underneath. The Golden Gate Bridge in San Francisco, USA, is a fine example.

The roadway of a suspension bridge hangs from cables slung from two towers. The distance between the towers is the bridge's main span. The longest suspension bridge is the Humber Bridge in England (1,410 m main span). By 1998 the Akashi Kaikyo bridge in Japan (1,780 m) will hold the suspension-bridge world record.

Below: The port of Rotterdam. In the late 1800s the New Waterway, a wide canal, was dug to allow large ships to enter the port from the North Sea. Rotterdam is now Europe's leading port for sea freight.

Left: San Francisco's Golden Gate Bridge was built in 1937. Its main span of 1,280 m is suspended from steel towers 227 m high. In high winds the road can safely sway 8 m from side to side.

Below: Three main types of bridge construction. ('Truss' is another term for 'beam' bridge.) The Forth Bridge, shown on page 46, is an example of the fourth type, the cantilever bridge. Each type of bridge can carry a roadway or railway.

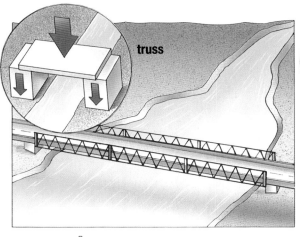

truss

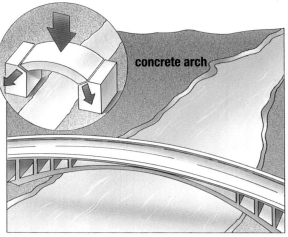

concrete arch

suspension

UNDERSEA TUNNELS

Japan has more transport tunnels than any other country. The Seikan Rail Tunnel is almost 54 km long, 23 km of which is under water. The longest tunnel in the world, it links Honshu and Hokkaido islands. Here the sea is about 140 m deep, and the tunnel lies 100 m below the seabed. It took 20 years to build the tunnel, which was completed in 1985, and the first trains began to use it in 1988.

Undersea tunnels need be no more difficult or expensive to build than land tunnels. Some are made by sinking giant tubes along the seabed. The Chesapeake Bay Tunnel in the USA was built like this. Other tunnels are bored by special machines, burrowing like giant moles through clay and rock.

EUROTUNNEL

Eurotunnel, linking Britain and France is almost 50 km in length, with 38 km of tunnel below the English Channel. It was dug by huge tunnel-boring machines, each weighing 1,300 tonnes, which moved forward at roughly 12 cm a minute. Behind them came a construction train, with a conveyor belt to remove the waste, and machinery to line the tunnel with concrete. The twin rail tunnels are 7.6 m in diameter. Between them is a smaller service tunnel. Huge pumps blow air into the service tunnel to ventilate the system.

Eurotunnel is for rail, not road traffic. Electric shuttle trains will carry people and vehicles through the twin tunnels. There will also be a high-speed rail link from London to Paris. After Eurotunnel opens in 1993, crossing the Channel may take 35 minutes.

Right: Eurotunnel shuttle trains will run between terminals at Folkestone and Calais. Trains will normally run in one direction only through each main tunnel. There are two crossover points for single working, when needed.

Below: Shuttle trains specially designed for the Channel tunnel will carry vehicles and their drivers and passengers inside enclosed railway wagons. Vehicles will drive along platforms beside the trains and load on special wagons at one end. They will unload from similar wagons at the other end of the trains.

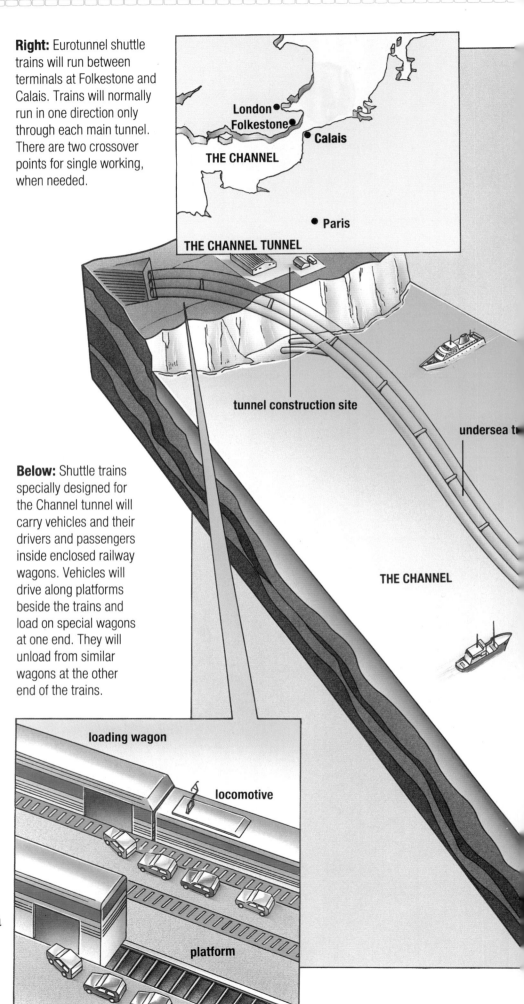

London
Folkestone
Calais
THE CHANNEL
Paris
THE CHANNEL TUNNEL

tunnel construction site

undersea t

THE CHANNEL

loading wagon

locomotive

platform

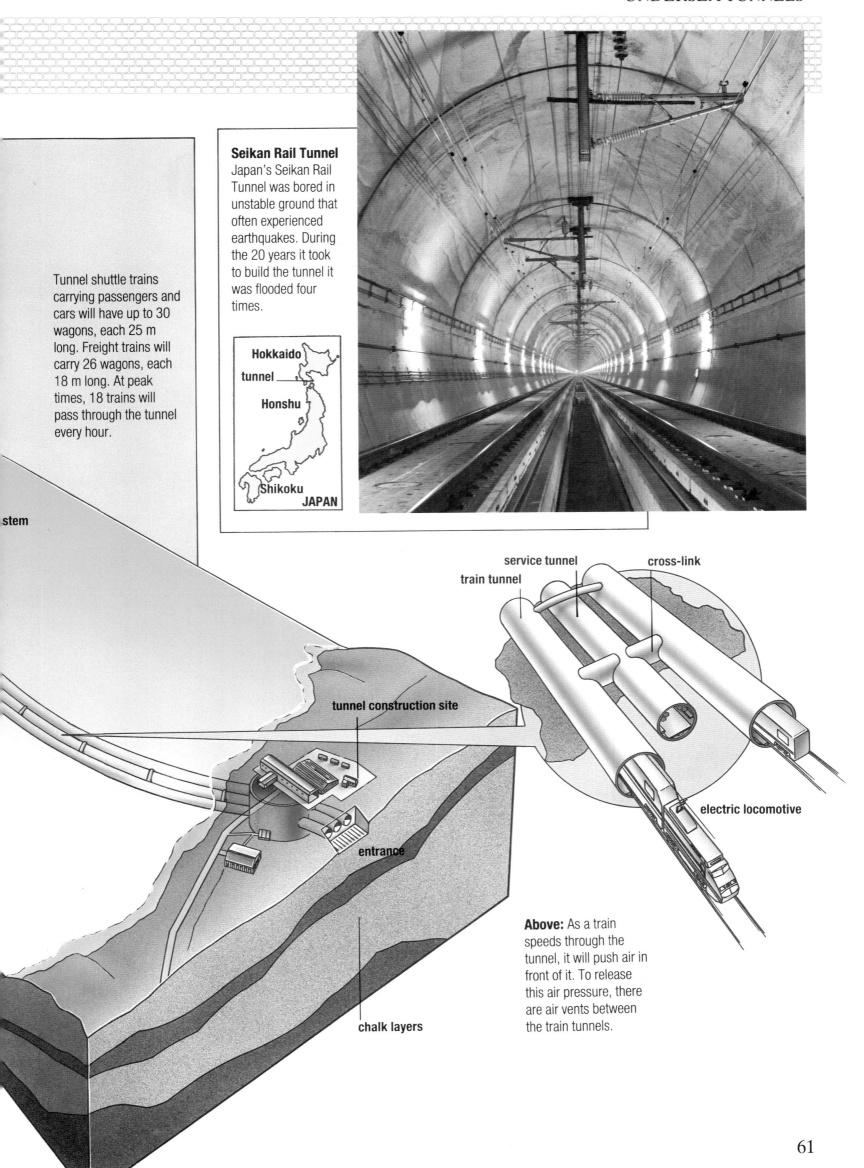

Seikan Rail Tunnel

Japan's Seikan Rail Tunnel was bored in unstable ground that often experienced earthquakes. During the 20 years it took to build the tunnel it was flooded four times.

Hokkaido

tunnel

Honshu

Shikoku

JAPAN

Tunnel shuttle trains carrying passengers and cars will have up to 30 wagons, each 25 m long. Freight trains will carry 26 wagons, each 18 m long. At peak times, 18 trains will pass through the tunnel every hour.

stem

service tunnel

train tunnel

cross-link

tunnel construction site

entrance

electric locomotive

chalk layers

Above: As a train speeds through the tunnel, it will push air in front of it. To release this air pressure, there are air vents between the train tunnels.

MOTORWAYS

Below: Highway construction involves bulldozers and earth-movers, ditch-diggers, paving machines to spread concrete or tarmac (asphalt) , and heavy rollers to make the road surface hard and smooth.

Using the Pan-American Highway, a motorist can drive almost all the way from Alaska in North America to the tip of South America. It is the world's longest road system – 26,000 km from end to end.

The USA has 6.5 million km of roads, more than any other country. This includes 688,000 km of freeways and superhighways (known as motorways in Britain). Yet, despite the Americans' love of cars and fast roads, motorways are not an American invention.

ROMAN ROADS TO MOTORWAYS
After the Ancient Romans, who built some 80,000 km of well-drained, stone-paved roads, medieval roads were scarcely fit for bullock carts. When automobiles first appeared, in the 1880s, the old dirt roads had to be hurriedly smoothed out and tarred over.

In the 1920s Italy built the first superhighways, the *autostradas*. These were fast roads that bypassed towns and avoided traffic jams. Later, other countries did the same. As the number of privately-owned cars increased, so more motorways, and bigger ones, were urgently needed.

Constructing a highway with six or eight lanes means shifting millions of tonnes of soil. Huge machines excavate and level the roadway and lay a concrete or tarmac surface. Bridges, tunnels, and interchanges, to ensure the smooth flow of traffic, also have to be built. The "smart" highways of tomorrow will have electronic detectors and radio links to warn drivers of any hold-ups ahead.

Right: Los Angeles has many overpasses, underpasses, and complex interchanges.

AIRPORTS

Perhaps, in 20 years' time airliners will land and take off near-vertically in city centres. But the planes of today need huge out-of-town airports such as London's Heathrow or Chicago's O'Hare, the busiest of all, where a plane arrives or leaves on average every 40 seconds or so.

A big airport is like a miniature city. Its "population" is made up of all the airport workers and airline passengers. Every newly-arrived wide-bodied jet unloads 200 or 300 more people. Hundreds of millions of passengers pass through the major airports every year.

HOW AIRPORTS EVOLVED

Until the 1950s most airports were grass fields, with a runway and a few small buildings. Today, even a medium-sized airport is 100 times bigger than the biggest railway station. The world's largest airport, King Khalid International in Saudi Arabia, covers an area of 221 sq km. Airports have big buildings as well as long runways. The terminal at Hartsfield Atlanta International in Georgia, USA, occupies 20 ha (the size of 20 football pitches).

In addition, warehouses, fuel stores, car parks, shops, hotels, and restaurants all require space, as does the nerve centre of the airport, the control tower. Large aircraft need runways 4,000 m long, with a further 2,000 m at either end as a safety precaution. Most airports have only one or two runways, but the new airport at Denver, Colorado, USA has 12. Planes also need taxi-ways, loading aprons, and service hangars, all of which must be provided for in planning a new airport.

Above: Planes lined up at Terminal 4, Heathrow. Heathrow is London's main airport and the world's busiest airport for international passenger traffic. London also has two other international airports, Gatwick and Stansted.

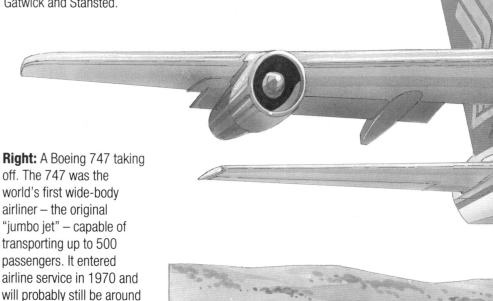

Right: A Boeing 747 taking off. The 747 was the world's first wide-body airliner – the original "jumbo jet" – capable of transporting up to 500 passengers. It entered airline service in 1970 and will probably still be around in the 21st century.

Right: John F. Kennedy International Airport in New York City ranks fifth among US airports in terms of passengers departing and arriving (over 28 million a year) and aircraft movements (255,000). New York City's two other main airports are Newark and La Guardia.

SKYSCRAPERS

The Messeturm in Frankfurt, Germany, is Europe's tallest building. It stands 256 m high and has 53 storeys. Yet, alongside the giant skyscrapers of the USA, it is a midget. The 110-storey Sears Tower in Chicago soars to 443 m and is currently the tallest building in the world. But that title will go to another Chicago skyscraper, the Miglin Beitler Tower, when it is completed. Known as the "Sky Needle", the 125-storey building will reach almost 600 m. In theory, there is no limit to how high a building can be.

HISTORY OF THE SKYSCRAPER

Architects and builders began reaching for the sky in the late 1800s. As the price of land in the city centres rose, they built upwards rather than outwards. A skyscraper is too massive to be supported by brick walls. Instead, it has a skeleton of steel girders or tubes. The outer skin can be brick, stone, or glass. The very first skyscraper, designed by William Jenney in Chicago in 1883, had only 19 storeys. But its metal-box design was revolutionary.

New York ruled the skyline from 1913, first with the Woolworth Building (60 storeys), and then from 1932 with the Empire State Building, whose 102 storeys stretch up 381 m. In 1973 New York was overtaken by Chicago with the Sears Tower (110 storeys).

A modern skyscraper weighs 350,000 tonnes or more. Yet, using today's construction methods, such giant buildings can be erected at amazing speed. The construction must allow for the building to sway by up to a metre in strong winds.

Above: Manhattan Island in New York City has more skyscrapers than any other city section in the world. The World Trade Center with its twin towers is the world's second-highest building.

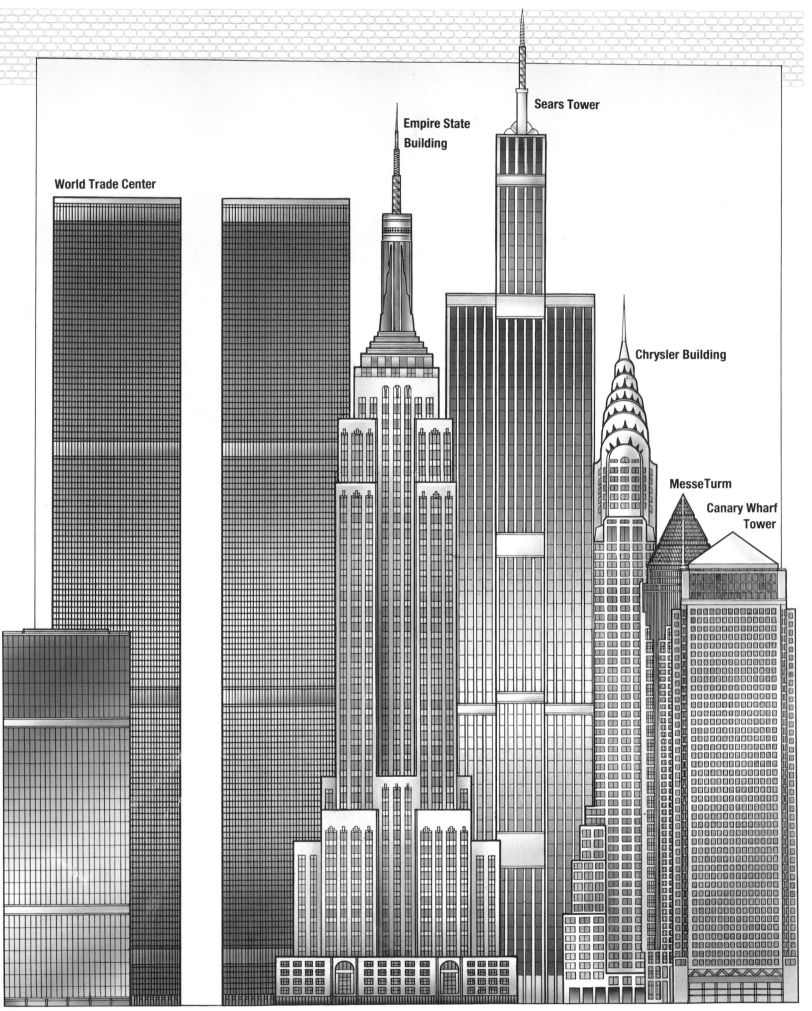

World Trade Center

Empire State Building

Sears Tower

Chrysler Building

MesseTurm

Canary Wharf Tower

Montparnasse

Above: Famous skyscrapers from around the world. Since the 102-storey Empire State Building was completed in 1931, the tallest skyscrapers have only increased in height by eight storeys or 62 m. But engineers believe it is possible to build a 1,000-storey skyscraper. The USA is home to the nine tallest skyscrapers in the world. The tallest in Europe is the MesseTurm. It is the 12th tallest.

POWER SYMBOLS

As buildings, the Houses of Parliament in London, the Kremlin in Moscow, and the Pentagon in Arlington, USA, would seem to have very little in common. But they are alike in that all three are centres and symbols of power.

The Pentagon is the US Defense Department's headquarters and one of the world's largest office buildings. It occupies 12 ha and each of its five sides is 281 m long. It accommodates a staff of 29,000, with parking space for 10,000 cars.

Britain's Houses of Parliament look much older than they are. The New Palace of Westminster, to give it its full name, was built between the 1830s and 1850s, after the medieval Parliament burned down. It includes the House of Commons, which was again rebuilt after World War II, and the House of Lords. The Victoria Tower, dating from 1858, is 102 m high, 5 m higher than the famous clock tower, whose 13.5-tonne bell Big Ben strikes the hours. Westminster Hall, built between 1097 and 1099, survived the fire of 1834, and, unlike the House of Commons, it escaped the bombs of World War II.

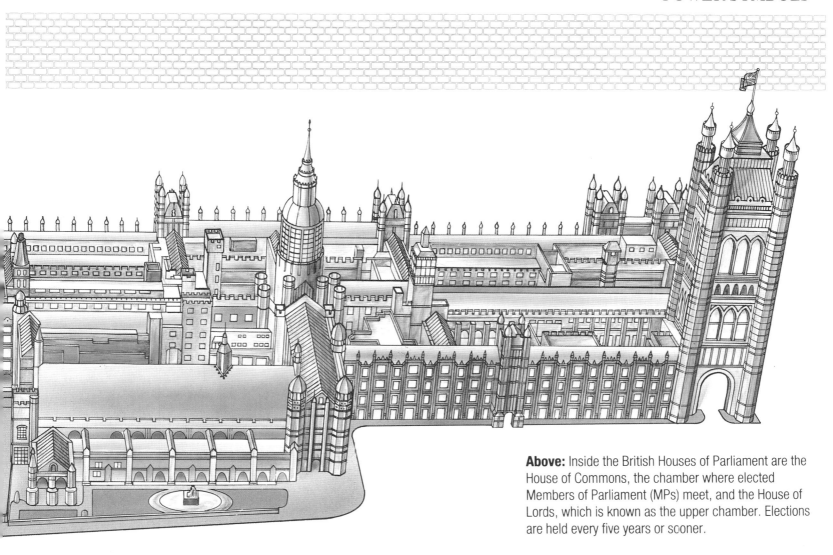

Above: Inside the British Houses of Parliament are the House of Commons, the chamber where elected Members of Parliament (MPs) meet, and the House of Lords, which is known as the upper chamber. Elections are held every five years or sooner.

Left: The Pentagon, from where the US armed forces – the most powerful in the world – are now controlled. Its shape and size make it an impressive symbol of the USA's military might. The Pentagon building was completed in 1943.

Right: The Kremlin in Moscow. It was originally a wooden fortress, built in 1156. The stone walls and towers were added in the 1300s. Once the heart of Soviet power, it now houses the Russian parliament.

From 1918 until recently, the Moscow Kremlin, meaning "fortress", was the heart of Soviet Communist power. Earlier, the tsars were crowned and buried there, and until 1712 when the capital moved from Moscow to St. Petersburg, it was the tsar's residence. The Kremlin dates from 1367 and occupies 36 ha. Inside the Kremlin's walled triangle with its 20 towers, are cathedrals and palaces, and the largest bell in the world, the 196-tonne Tsar Kolokol, which has never been rung since it was cast in 1733.

SPECIAL BUILDINGS

From time to time, architects and construction engineers are asked to build something special, for instance, a stadium for 200,000 sports fans, or a workshop big enough to put a Moon rocket inside, or a very tall tower.

The Canadian National Tower in Toronto is 553 m high, nearly double the Eiffel Tower's 300 m. Its slender pinnacle of concrete and steel stands on the biggest concrete raft foundation ever made. Cranes were used to hoist construction materials as high as 450 m, but above that a helicopter was needed. The tower was finished in 1976, three years after work began.

Sports stadia are some of the most spectacular buildings in the world. Most of them are open bowls, like the Maracana Stadium in Rio de Janeiro, Brazil. The world's largest stadium is the Strahov in Czechoslovakia, which can hold a capacity crowd of 240,000. The stadium built for the 1972 Olympic Games in Munich, Germany, has a vast tent-like canopy hung from cables, the biggest ever built. Impressive sports arenas with roofs include the Toronto SkyDome (1989), which has a sliding retractable roof.

WORLD'S BIGGEST WORKSHOP
The Vehicle Assembly Building (VAB) at Cape Canaveral, Florida, USA, is huge: 218 m long, 158 m wide, and 160 m high. Built in the 1960s, it housed the 111-m tall Saturn-5 rockets that launched the Apollo astronauts to the Moon. Today Space Shuttles are prepared inside the VAB, from where a giant tracked crawler moves the spacecraft to the launch pad.

Above: An aerial view of the Maracana Stadium in Rio de Janeiro. This huge bowl-shaped arena can seat 155,000 soccer fans with room for 55,000 more spectators standing.

Left: The CN Tower in Toronto is the tallest self-supporting tower in the world. It contains 130,000 tonnes of reinforced concrete. Near the top in the Sky Pod is a revolving restaurant. On the very top is a radio mast.

Right: The Vehicle Assembly Building at Kennedy Space Center, Cape Canaveral. The building has a floor area about the size of five soccer pitches. VAB's doors are so high that the Statue of Liberty could be moved inside with 40 m to spare.

HIGH TECHNOLOGY

Modern high technology can produce unusual new buildings as well as additions – often controversial – to traditional buildings that are part of the familiar city landscape.

Built between 1981 and 1985, the Hong Kong and Shanghai Bank in Hong Kong is a most unusual office building. Its floors hang from eight steel masts. This design provides extra working space, an important consideration when building land is very expensive. It also creates an atrium – a space open to the sky – within the building.

INSIDE OUTSIDE

Some modern architects have chosen to put the "insides" of the building on the outside. The Pompidou Centre, an arts centre in Paris, looks unfinished. It has been like this since 1977. What you see is the "works" of the building. A network of pipes and tubes carry the services or "life support" systems – power, water, air conditioning, heating, and telecommunications. Lifts, escalators, and staircases are on the outside, glass walls on the inside. Not everyone likes the design, but it provides a lot of internal floor space for displays and people.

Also in Paris is the Louvre. Built mainly in Renaissance style, it was once a royal palace. Today it is one of the world's most famous art museums. In 1989, a futuristic addition appeared in the square outside the Louvre. This was a 20-m glass pyramid, the creation of the architect I.M. Pei, which serves as an entrance to the museum. Now, old and new – Louvre and pyramid – together greet the unsuspecting visitor.

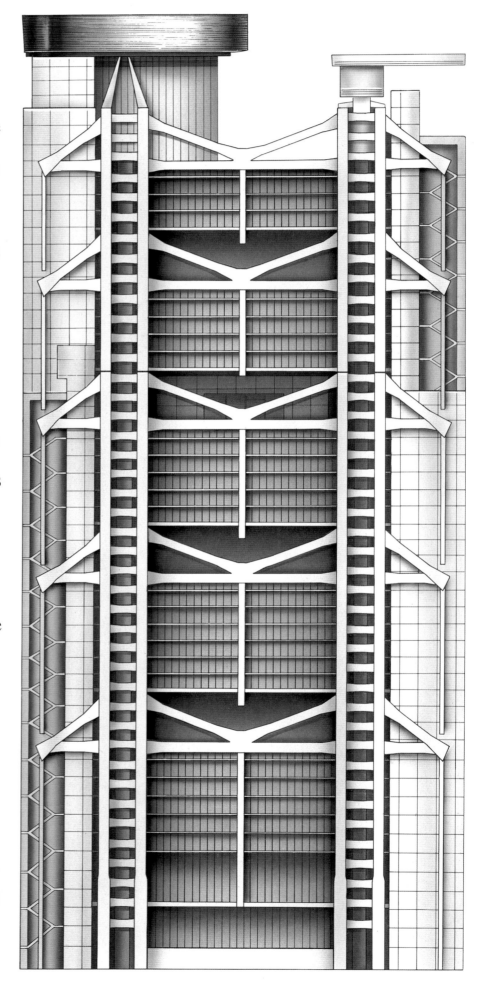

Right: The Pompidou Centre, Paris. The outside looks a jumble of coloured pipes and tubes. Inside, the wide floor space serves as an arts centre, museum, and library.

Left: The Hong Kong and Shanghai Bank's headquarters in Hong Kong was designed to squeeze as much space as possible onto a small ground site.

Below: The Pei Pyramid in the Cour Napoléon, Paris. By day, or floodlit at night, the glass pyramid makes people stop and look, drawing them to the Louvre.

AMAZING SHAPES

Above: The Opera House stands on Bennelong Point in Sydney harbour. Beneath the distinctive sail-like roofs are three concert halls and a restaurant.

Most modern skyscrapers are glass-walled slabs. You could turn one upside-down, say the critics, and no one would know the difference. But not all modern buildings are so simple. Since the 1950s new construction techniques have given architects freedom to create some amazing shapes, and new materials – plastics, glass fibres, and ceramics – have presented them with fresh and exciting challenges.

New York's Guggenheim Museum, designed by Frank Lloyd Wright and built between 1956 and 1959, looks like a giant bottle screw cap. The geodesic dome, invented by another American, Buckminster Fuller, resembles a bubble-shaped Moon base. On the Opera House beside Sydney harbour, Australia, each roof shell looks like a billowing white sail on a yacht. The building was completed in 1973.

Some amazing shapes built on a large scale are purely functional. For example, the world's largest tidal barrier, across the River Thames in London, and North Sea oil platforms, large enough to fill a city square, are working structures.

Above: The Tree House in Rotterdam, Netherlands. Much modern housing is dull. Yet a house can look interesting, enhance its environment, and still be an efficient and comfortable place for people to live in.

Left: Skyline of St. Louis, USA, with Gateway Arch standing on the bank of the Mississippi River.

Many other amazing shapes are wholly or partly for fun. A hotel at the Disney Epcot Center in Florida (the world's biggest entertainment resort) with two 17-m-long model dolphins on its roof, is an obvious example.

The Pontiac Silverdome in Michigan, its glass-fibre roof held up by air pressure, and the 192-m high Gateway to the West arch in St. Louis, Missouri are each marvels of technology. Even a modern family home can be a small wonder: energy-efficient, fun to live in, and fun to look at too.

INDEX

ACKNOWLEDGEMENTS

All major illustrations by John James
All diagrammatic artwork and maps by Hayward Art Group.

Photographs as follows (t=top, b=bottom, l=left, r=right):
Pages 10, 13, 15, 16-17 Zefa. 17t S & O Mathews. 18 Zefa. 19 The Hutchison Library/Pierrette Collomb. 20, 21, 23, 25, 26, 27, 28 Zefa. 31 Michael Holford. 32, 33, 32, 36, 37, 39, 40. 41, 42, 43 Zefa. 44t The Hutchison Library/Bernard Regent. 44b The Hutchison Library/Bernard GËrard. 45, 46, 47 Zefa. 48 The Hutchison Library/Camerpix. 49, 50, 51 Zefa. 52-53 Mary Evans Picture Library. 53, 54, 55 Zefa. 56 The Hutchison Library. 57, 58, 59 Zefa. 61 Japan Railway Construction Corporation. 62-63, 64, 65, 66, 68, 69, 70, 71l Zefa. 71r TRH Pictures. 73, 74, 75 Zefa.